Nat's Cap

by Andrew Lunn
illustrated by Len Epstein

Core Decodable 19

McGraw Hill Education

Bothell, WA • Chicago, IL • Columbus, OH • New York, NY

MHEonline.com

Send all inquiries to:
McGraw-Hill Education
8787 Orion Place
Columbus, OH 43240

ISBN: 978-0-02-132763-8
MHID: 0-02-132763-7

Printed in China

6 7 8 9 10 DSS 27 26 25 24 23

Nat has a cap.

Can Mom stop Nat's cap?

Mom can't stop Nat's cap.

A cab can't stop Nat's cap.

Can Nat's cap stop?

A cat can stop Nat's cap!